## Mel Bay's

# THE DULCIMER SONGBOOK

### by
### Bud Ford and Donna Ford

# ACKNOWLEDGEMENTS

This book is dedicated to Buddy and Erin Ford whose smiles and laughter make life a song.

Special thanks to Ruby Baxter, Gherald and Jennie Ford, Nellie Wallace, Tim, Tony and Lynn Carnahan for their help, patience and understanding.

Photographic setting: Rockey's Storybook Studio, Manitou Springs, Colorado. Sculpture by Charles Rockey.

1 2 3 4 5 6 7 8 9 0

# TABLE OF CONTENTS

EXPLANATION OF TABLATURE . . . . . . . . . . . . . . . . . . . . . . . . . . . . . . 3
EXPLANATION OF IONIAN, DORIAN, AEOLIAN AND MIXOLYDIAN TUNING  4

ALL THROUGH THE NIGHT . . . . . . . . . . . . . . . . . . . . . . . . . . . . . . . 6
ARKANSAS TRAVELER . . . . . . . . . . . . . . . . . . . . . . . . . . . . . . 8
ASH GROVE (THE) . . . . . . . . . . . . . . . . . . . . . . . . . . . . . . . . .10
AURA LEE . . . . . . . . . . . . . . . . . . . . . . . . . . . . . . . . . . . . .12

BANKS OF THE OHIO . . . . . . . . . . . . . . . . . . . . . . . . . . . . . . .14
BATTLE HYMN OF THE REPUBLIC . . . . . . . . . . . . . . . . . . . . . . . .16
BIG ROCK CANDY MOUNTAIN . . . . . . . . . . . . . . . . . . . . . . . . . .18
BILE 'DEM CABBAGE DOWN . . . . . . . . . . . . . . . . . . . . . . . . . . .20
BLACK IS THE COLOR . . . . . . . . . . . . . . . . . . . . . . . . . . . . . .22
BLUETAIL FLY . . . . . . . . . . . . . . . . . . . . . . . . . . . . . . . . . . .24

CARELESS LOVE . . . . . . . . . . . . . . . . . . . . . . . . . . . . . . . . . .26
CLEMENTINE . . . . . . . . . . . . . . . . . . . . . . . . . . . . . . . . . . . .28
CRAWDAD SONG . . . . . . . . . . . . . . . . . . . . . . . . . . . . . . . . . .30
CUMBERLAND GAP . . . . . . . . . . . . . . . . . . . . . . . . . . . . . . . .32

DARLIN' COREY . . . . . . . . . . . . . . . . . . . . . . . . . . . . . . . . . .34
DRILL YE TARRIERS . . . . . . . . . . . . . . . . . . . . . . . . . . . . . . .36
DRUNKEN SAILOR . . . . . . . . . . . . . . . . . . . . . . . . . . . . . . . . .38

EVERY NIGHT . . . . . . . . . . . . . . . . . . . . . . . . . . . . . . . . . . . .40

THE FOGGY, FOGGY DEW . . . . . . . . . . . . . . . . . . . . . . . . . . . . .42
FROGGIE WENT A-COURTIN' . . . . . . . . . . . . . . . . . . . . . . . . . . .44

GOLDEN SLIPPERS . . . . . . . . . . . . . . . . . . . . . . . . . . . . . . . . .46
GO TELL IT ON THE MOUNTAIN . . . . . . . . . . . . . . . . . . . . . . . . .50
GRANDFATHER'S CLOCK . . . . . . . . . . . . . . . . . . . . . . . . . . . . .52

I'VE GOT PEACE LIKE A RIVER . . . . . . . . . . . . . . . . . . . . . . . . .56

LONDONDERRY AIRE . . . . . . . . . . . . . . . . . . . . . . . . . . . . . . .58

OH MARY DON'T YOU WEEP . . . . . . . . . . . . . . . . . . . . . . . . . . .62
OLD ROSIN THE BEAU . . . . . . . . . . . . . . . . . . . . . . . . . . . . . .64
ON TOP OF OLD SMOKEY . . . . . . . . . . . . . . . . . . . . . . . . . . . . .66

RIDDLE SONG . . . . . . . . . . . . . . . . . . . . . . . . . . . . . . . . . . . .68

SALLY GODDIN . . . . . . . . . . . . . . . . . . . . . . . . . . . . . . . . . . .70
SCARBOROUGH FAIR . . . . . . . . . . . . . . . . . . . . . . . . . . . . . . .72
SHADY GROVE . . . . . . . . . . . . . . . . . . . . . . . . . . . . . . . . . . .74
SOLDIER'S JOY . . . . . . . . . . . . . . . . . . . . . . . . . . . . . . . . . . .76

THERE IS A BALM IN GILEAD . . . . . . . . . . . . . . . . . . . . . . . . . .78
THE WATER IS WIDE . . . . . . . . . . . . . . . . . . . . . . . . . . . . . . .80
WABASH CANNONBALL . . . . . . . . . . . . . . . . . . . . . . . . . . . . . .82

WILDWOOD FLOWER . . . . . . . . . . . . . . . . . . . . . . . . . . . . . . .84
WHEN THE SAINTS GO MARCHING IN . . . . . . . . . . . . . . . . . . . . .86

# Explanation of Tablature and Tuning

All of the songs in this book are written two ways: one simple version showing the single note melody for traditional playing as well as chords and words. The other version is designed for full style finger playing.

PLEASE NOTE: When a song has a fret number with a line over it you will be playing the bass drone as part of the melody.

The tablature used is very simple to read. The bottom line shows the position of the thumb on the melody strings. The middle line shows the position of the ring and/or middle finger on the treble drone with the upper line the position of the index finger on the bass drone.

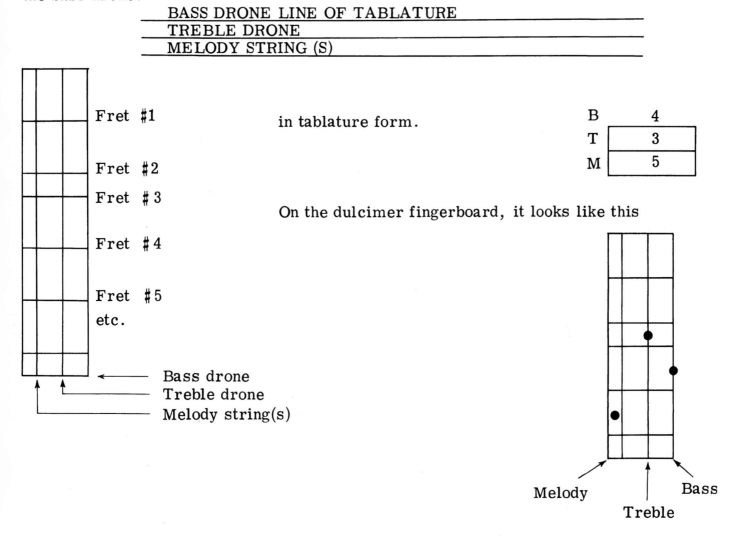

BASS DRONE LINE OF TABLATURE
TREBLE DRONE
MELODY STRING (S)

Fret #1    in tablature form.

Fret #2

Fret #3    On the dulcimer fingerboard, it looks like this

Fret #4

Fret #5
etc.

← Bass drone
Treble drone
Melody string(s)

| B | 4 |
|---|---|
| T | 3 |
| M | 5 |

Melody    Bass
Treble

Read the full tablature using the numbered finger positions while strumming across all the strings. This gives you a full melody along with a harmony pattern.

Use just the chord symbols and charts to play a simple chord background while singing the melody. The chord letter names and music also work for other instruments.

The four tunings used in this songbook are the Ionian, Aeolian, Dorian and Mixolydian. To determine the correct tuning for each song refer to the top right hand side of each song.

As the tunings vary, the same finger pattern may have a different name. For this reason, the actual finger pattern along with the proper names for the particular tuning are shown.

# Ionian Tuning

1. Tune the fourth string (Bass Drone) to the key note for the song.

2. Depress the bass drone just behind the fourth fret.
   Pluck the string and listen carefully to this sound.

3. Tune the third string (Treble drone) and the first and second strings (Melody strings) to this pitch.

4. With the bass drone depressed at the fourth fret, all four strings should sound the same.

If you have a three string dulcimer, your first string is the melody string corresponding to strings one and two on the four string.

If you have a broken string, strings one, two and three are usually plain strings from .010 to .014 and the fourth string a wound string from .018 to .028. These can be purchased from any music store. Long neck banjo or guitar strings are best.

# Dorian Tuning

The Dorian scale starts on the fourth fret.

1. Tune the Bass Drone to the key note for the song.

2. Depress the Bass Drone at the third fret. Play and listen carefully. Tune the first and second strings to this pitch.

3. Depress the Bass Drone at the fourth fret and tune the Treble Drone to this pitch.

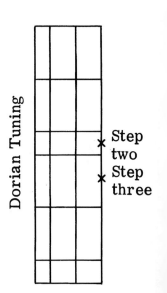

# Aeolian Tuning

The Aeolian scale starts on fret number one.

1. Tune the Bass Drone to the key note for the song.

2. Depress the Bass Drone on the 6th fret. Play and listen carefully.

3. Tune strings one and two to this pitch.

4. Depress the Bass Drone on the fourth fret. Tune the Treble Drone to this pitch.

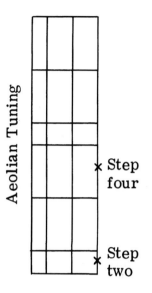

# Mixolydian Tuning

The Mixolydian scale starts on the open string.

1. Tune the Bass Drone to the key note for the song.

2. Depress the Bass Drone on the 7th fret. Play and listen carefully.

3. Tune strings one and two to this pitch.

4. Depress the Bass Drone on the fourth fret. Tune the Treble Drone to this pitch.

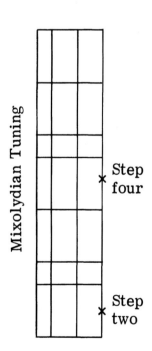

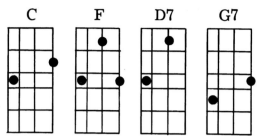

# ALL THROUGH THE NIGHT

Ionian Mode

Sleep, my child and peace at - tend thee

all through the night Guard - an an - gels

God will send thee, All through the night.

Soft the drow - sy hours are creep - ing,

Hill and vale in slum - ber sleep - ing' I my lov - ing

vig - il keep - ing, All through the night.

# ALL THROUGH THE NIGHT
## SOLO

Ionian Mode

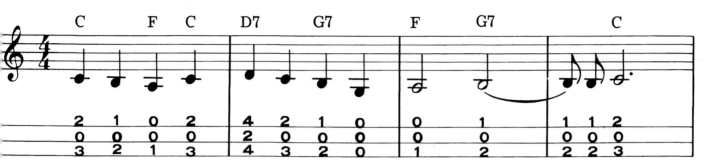

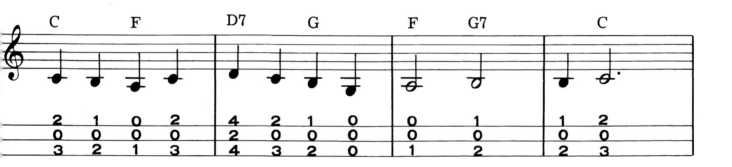

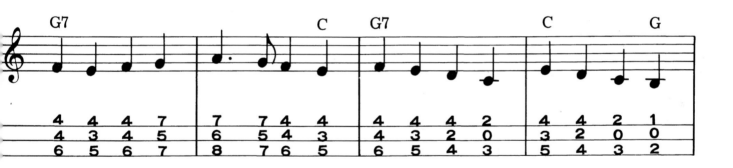

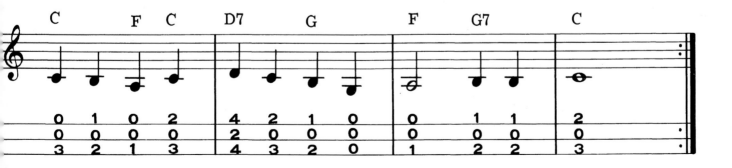

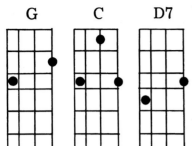

# ARKANSAS TRAVELER

Ionian Mode

# ARKANSAS TRAVELER
## SOLO

Ionian Mode

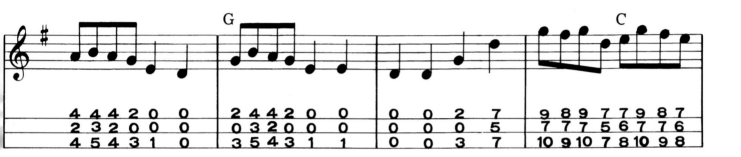

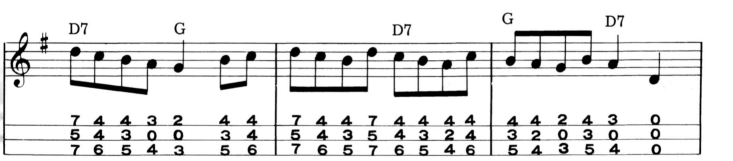

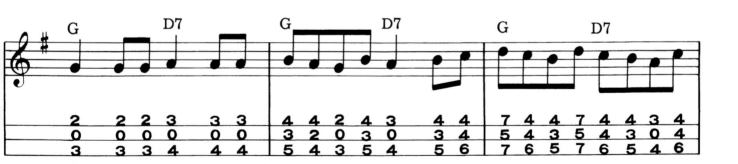

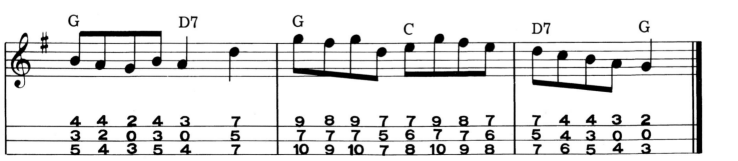

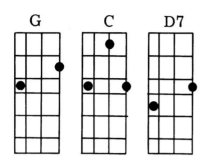

# ASH GROVE

Ionian Mode

# ASH GROVE
## SOLO

Ionian Mode

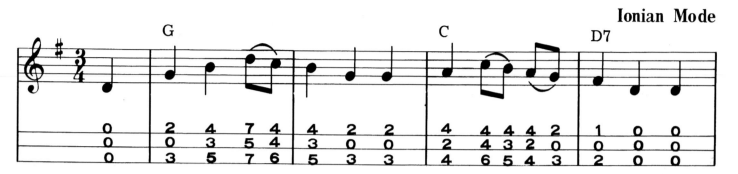

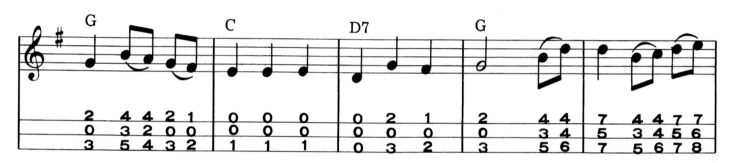

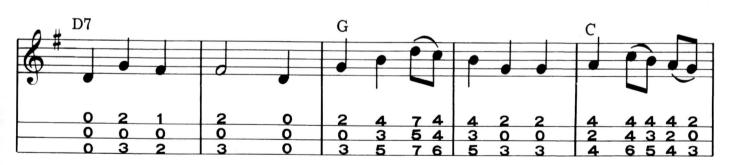

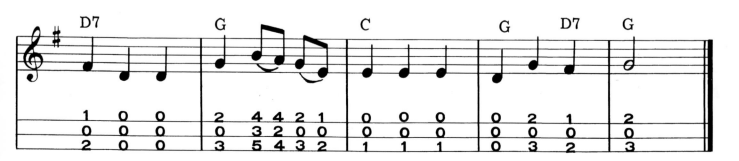

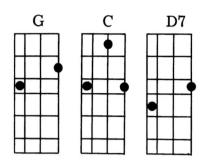

# AURA LEE

Ionian Mode

As the Black-Bird in the Spring, By the wil-low tree.____

Sat and piped I heard him sing of thee, my Au-ra Lee.

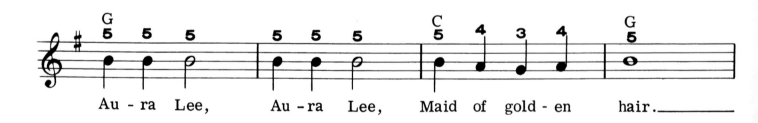

Au-ra Lee, Au-ra Lee, Maid of gold-en hair.____

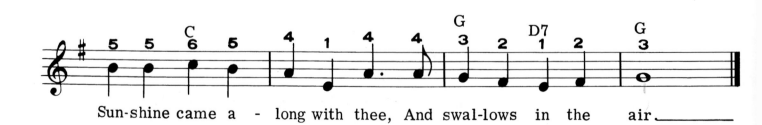

Sun-shine came a-long with thee, And swal-lows in the air.____

# AURA LEE
## SOLO

Ionian Mode

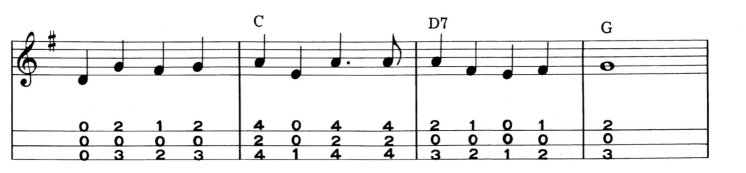

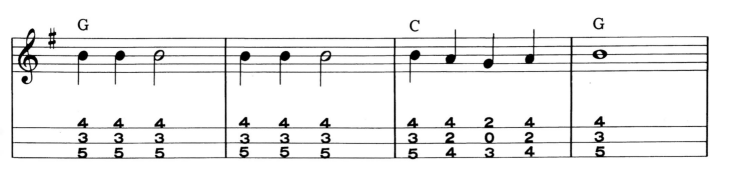

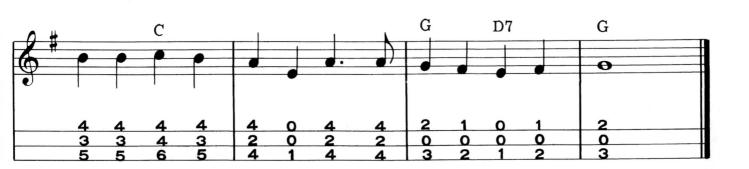

13

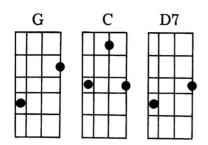

# BANKS OF THE OHIO

Ionian Mode

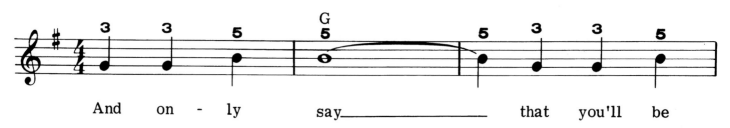

And on - ly say_____ that you'll be

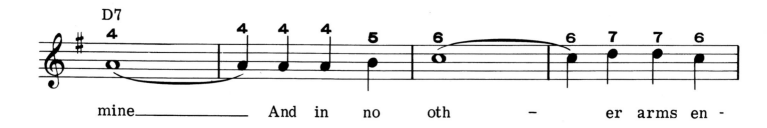

mine_____ And in no oth – er arms en -

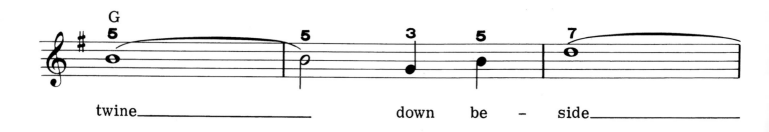

twine_____ down be – side_____

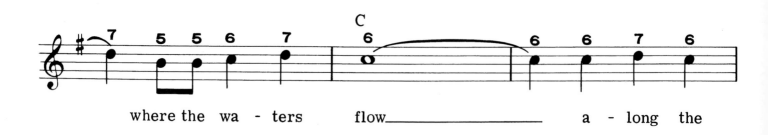

where the wa - ters flow_____ a - long the

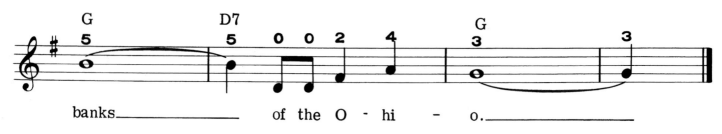

banks_____ of the O - hi - o._____

# BANKS OF THE OHIO
## SOLO

Ionian Mode

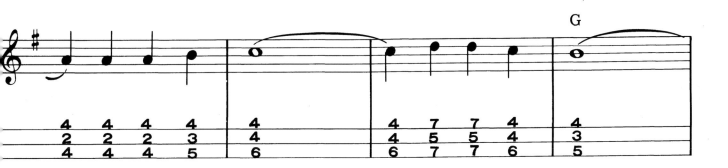

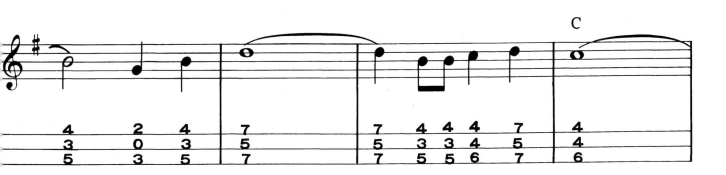

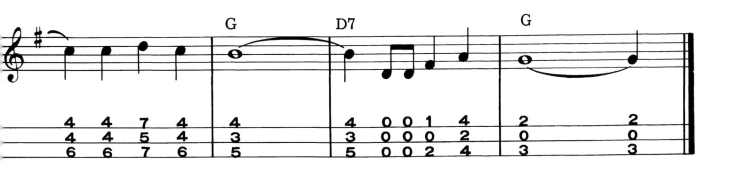

# BATTLE HYMN
# OF THE REPUBLIC

Ionian Mode

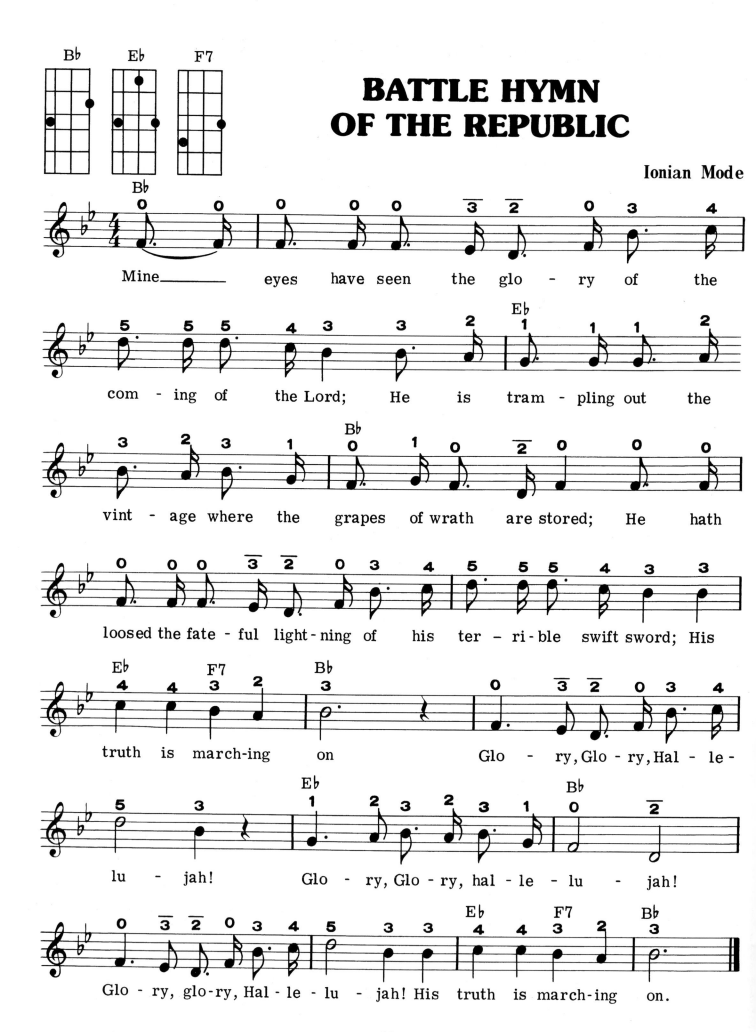

# BATTLE HYMN OF THE REPUBLIC
## SOLO

Ionian Mode

# BIG ROCK CANDY MOUNTAIN

Ionian Mode

On a sum-mer' day in the month of May. A___ bur-ly bum came hik-ing. Down a shad-y lane, through the sug-ar cane, He was Look-ing for his lik-ing. As he strolled a-long he sang this song, of the land of milk and hon-ey, Where a bum can stay for man-y a day, And he won't need an-y mon-ey. Oh, the buzz-in' of the bees in the Bub-ble Gum Trees. The so-da wa-ter foun-tain, By the lemon-ade Springs where the blue-bird sings, In the Big Rock Can-dy Moun-tain.

18

# BIG ROCK CANDY MOUNTAIN
## SOLO

Ionian Mode

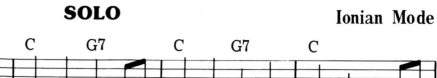
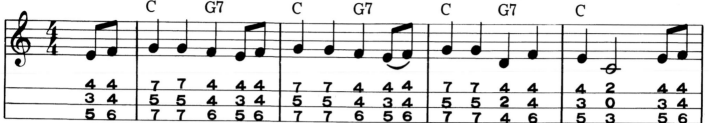
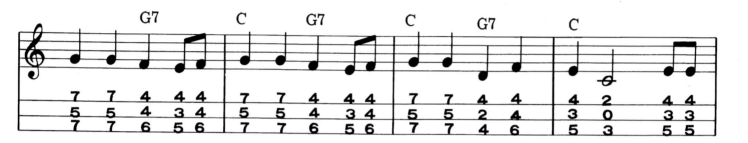
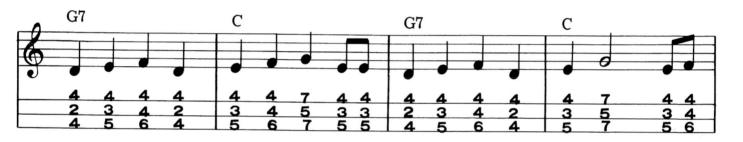
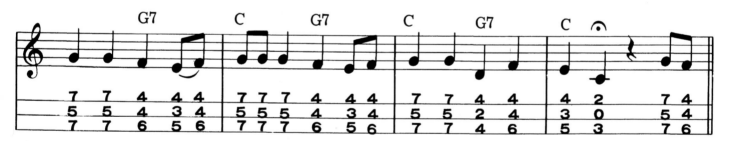
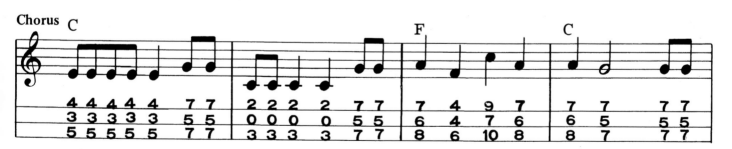
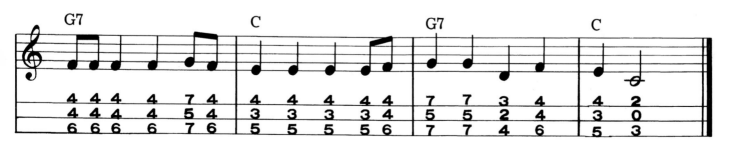

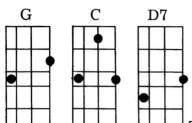

# BILE 'DEM CABBAGE DOWN

Tune Bass String to G

Ionian Mode

Bile' dem cab - bage   down,       bake' dat hoe cake   brown,       the

on - ly  song that   I  can sing  is  Bile' dem cab - bage   down.

# BILE 'DEM CABBAGE DOWN
## SOLO

Ionian Mode

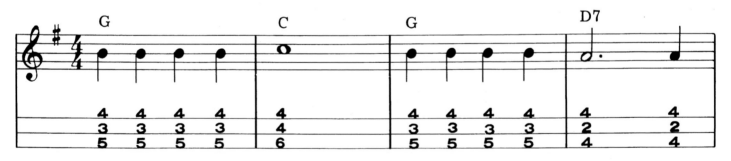

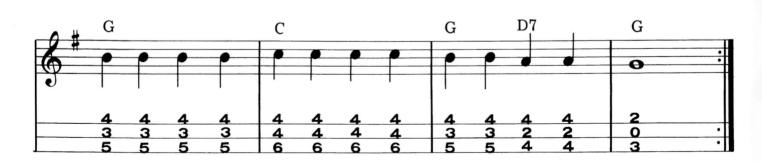

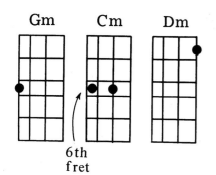

# BLACK IS THE COLOR

Aeolian Mode

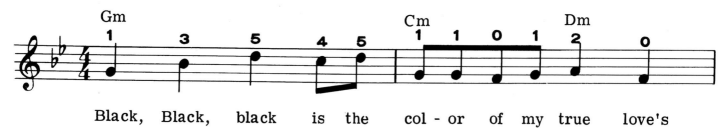

Black, Black, black is the col - or of my true love's

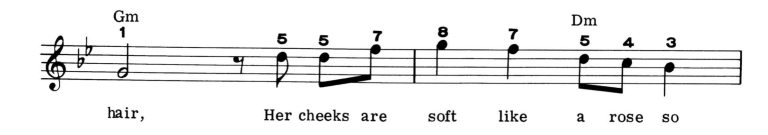

hair, Her cheeks are soft like a rose so

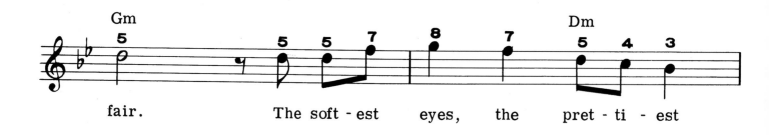

fair. The soft - est eyes, the pret - ti - est

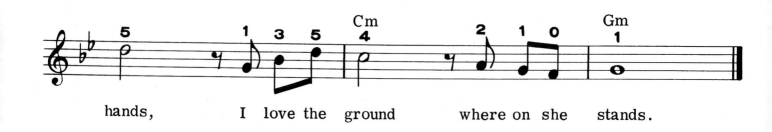

hands, I love the ground where on she stands.

# BLACK IS THE COLOR
## SOLO

Aeolian Mode

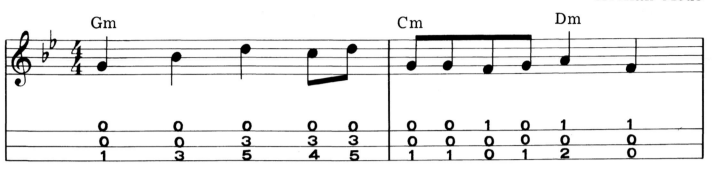

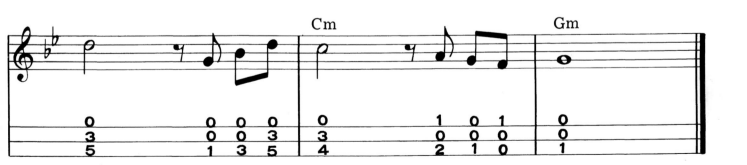

# BLUETAIL FLY

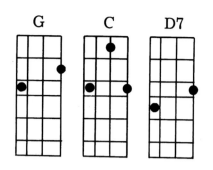

Ionian Mode

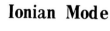

When I was young I used to wait on

Mas - ter and fetch him his plate, and pass the bot - tle when

he got dry, And brush a - way the blue - tail fly.

**Chorus**

Jim-my Crack Corn, and I don't care, Jim - my Crack Corn, and

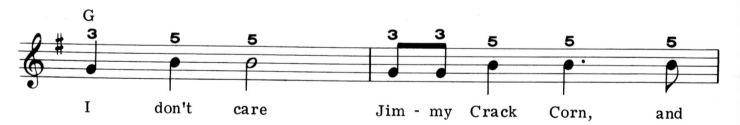

I don't care Jim - my Crack Corn, and

I don't care, my mas - ter's gone a - way.____

# BLUETAIL FLY
## SOLO

Ionian Mode

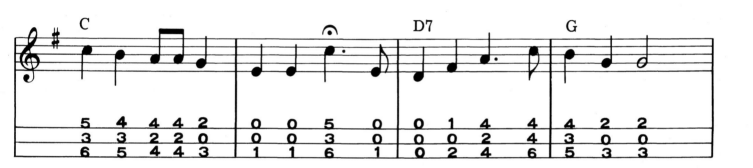

**Chorus**

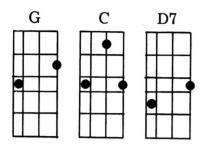

# CARELESS LOVE

Ionian Mode

Love, oh love, oh care-less love._____

Love, oh love, oh care-less love._____

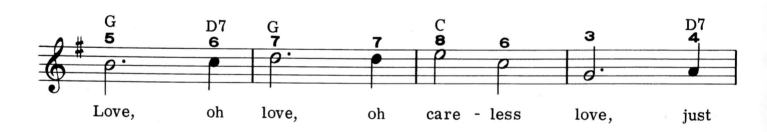

Love, oh love, oh care - less love, just

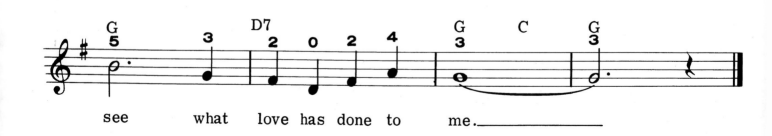

see what love has done to me._____

# CARELESS LOVE
## SOLO

Ionian Mode

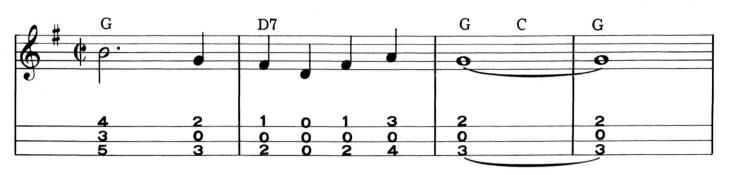

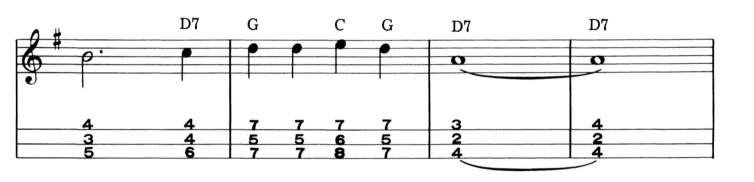

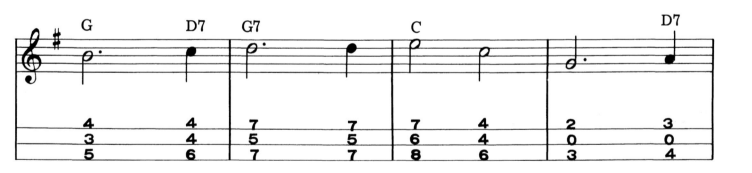

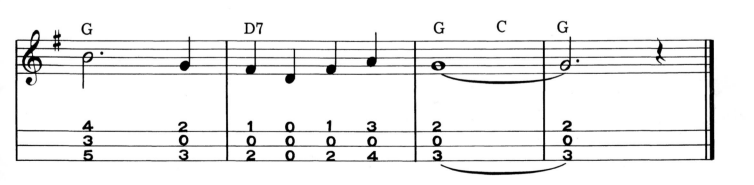

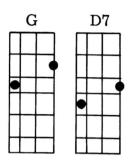

# CLEMENTINE

Ionian Mode

In a ca - vern, in a can yon, ex - ca -

va - ting for a mine, lived a min - er, for - ty

min - er, and his daugh - ter, Clem-en - tine.

**Chorus**

Oh, my dar - ling, Oh, my dar - ling, Oh, my

dar - ling, Clem-en - tine, you are lost and gone for -

ev - er, Dread-ful sor - ry, Clem-en - tine.

# CLEMENTINE
## SOLO

Ionian Mode

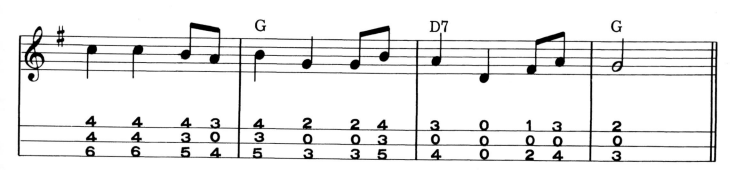

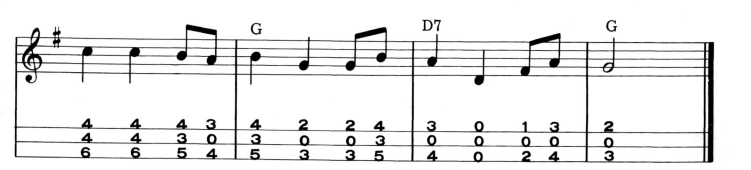

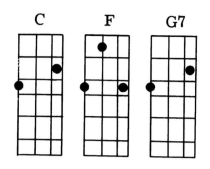

# CRAWDAD SONG

Ionian Mode

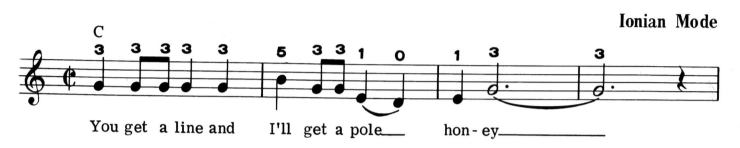

You get a line and I'll get a pole__ hon - ey_____

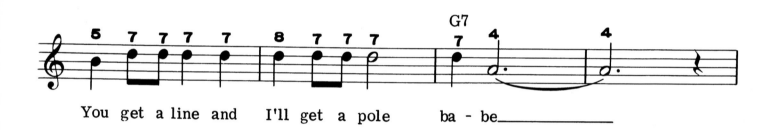

You get a line and I'll get a pole ba - be_____

You get a line and I'll get a pole, We'll go down to the

Craw-dad hole hon-ey, Sug-ar Bab - y mine._____

# CRAWDAD SONG
## SOLO

Ionian Mode

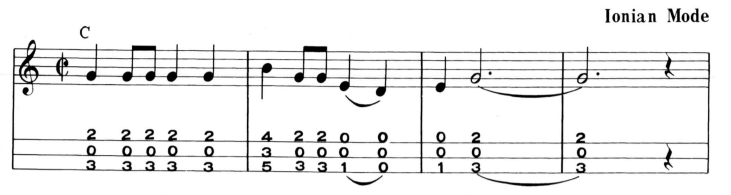

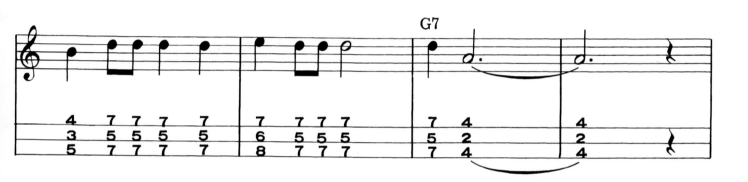

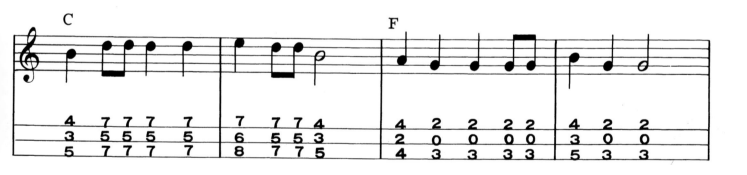

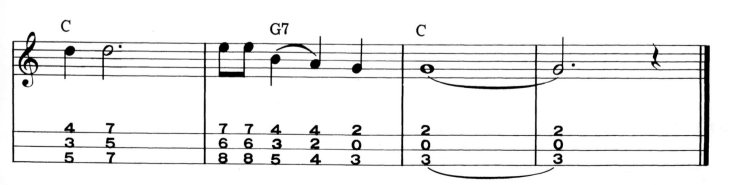

# CUMBERLAND GAP

Ionian Mode

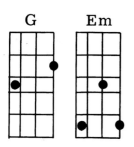

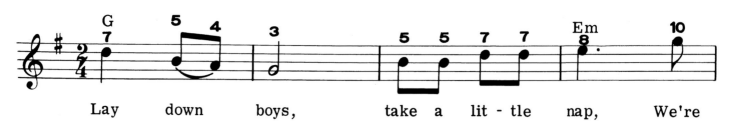

Lay down boys, take a lit - tle nap, We're

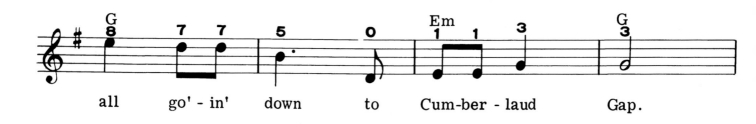

all go' - in' down to Cum-ber - laud Gap.

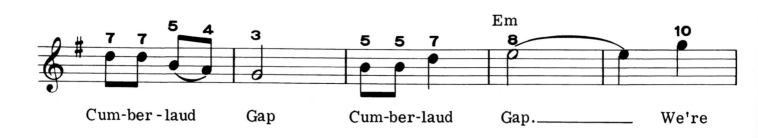

Cum-ber - laud Gap Cum-ber-laud Gap._____ We're

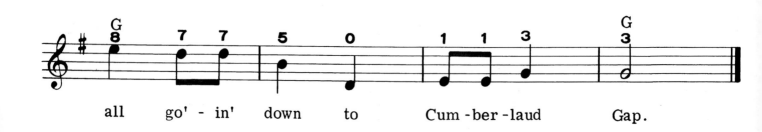

all go' - in' down to Cum -ber -laud Gap.

# CUMBERLAND GAP
## SOLO

Ionian Mode

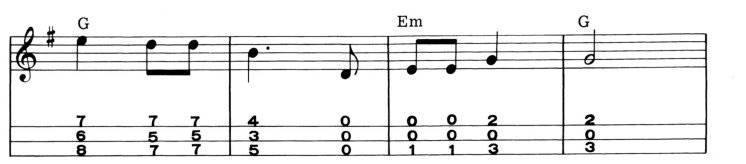

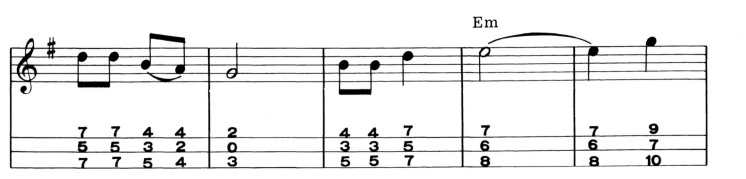

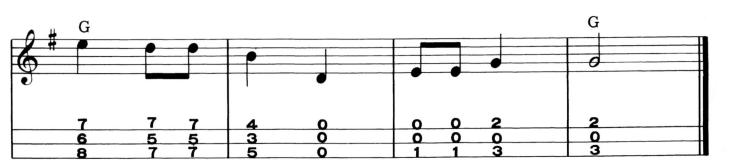

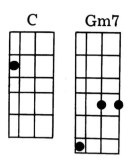

# DARLIN' COREY

Mixolydian Mode

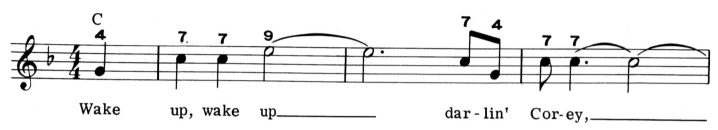

Wake up, wake up        dar-lin' Cor-ey,

—       what makes you sleep so sound? The—

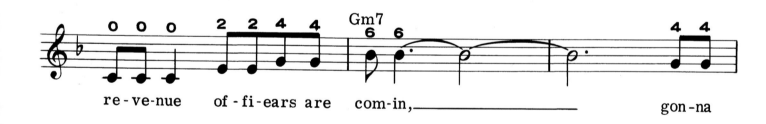

re-ve-nue of-fi-ears are com-in,         gon-na

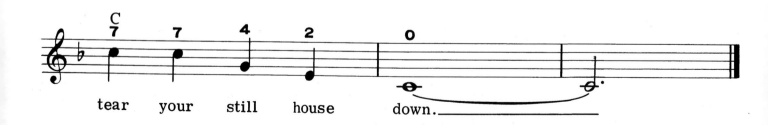

tear your still house down.

# DARLIN' COREY
## SOLO

Mixolydian Mode

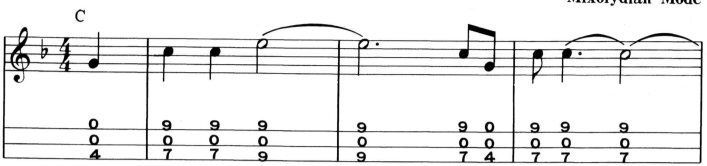

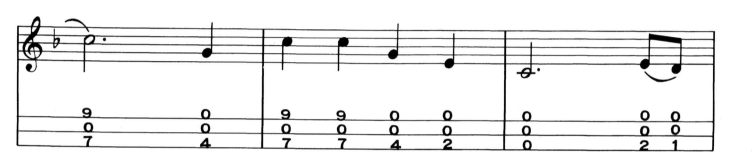

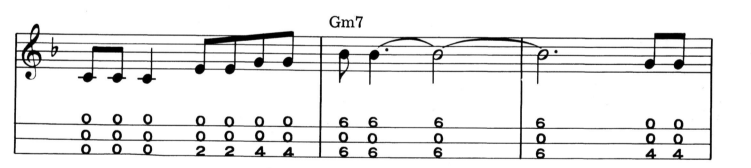

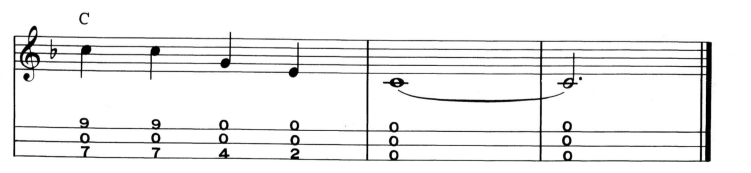

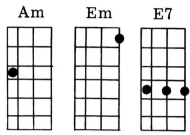

# DRILL YE TARRIERS

Aeolian Mode

Ev - 'ry morn - ing at sev - en o' - clock There were

twen - ty tar - ri - ers a - work - ing at the rock, And the

boss comes a - round and he says, "Keep still, And come down heav - y on the

east iron drill, "And drill, ye tar - ri - ers, drill.

Chorus

Drill, ye tar - ri - ers, drill, For it's work all day for the

su - gar in your tay, Down be - hind the rail - way, And

drill, ye tar - ri - ers, drill, and blast, and fire.____

# DRILL YE TARRIERS
## SOLO

Aeolian Mode

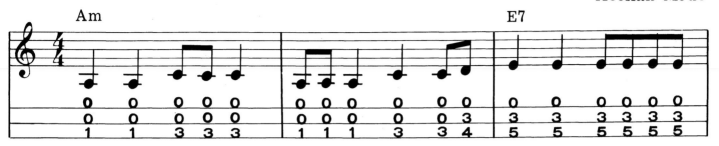

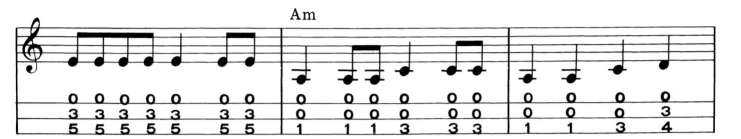

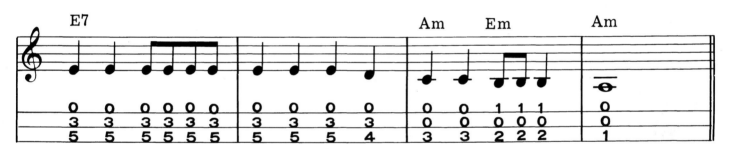

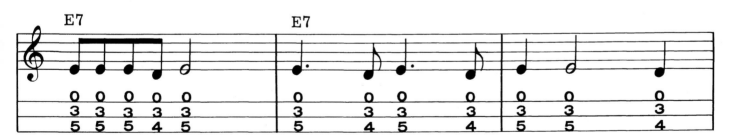

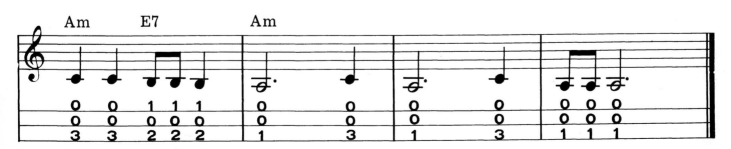

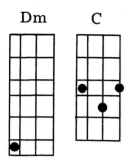

# DRUNKEN SAILOR

Dorian Mode

What shall we do with the Drunk - en Sail - or,

What shall we do with the Drunk-en Sail - or    What shall we do with the

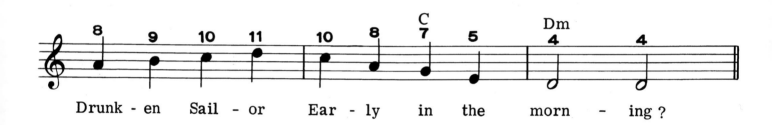

Drunk - en Sail - or    Ear - ly    in    the    morn - ing ?

**Chorus**

Aye,    aye    and    up she ris - es,    Aye,    aye    and    up she ris - es,

Aye,    aye    and    up she ris - es,    Ear - ly    in    the    morn - ing.

38

# DRUNKEN SAILOR
## SOLO

Dorian Mode

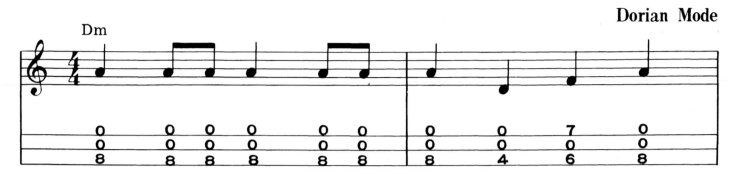

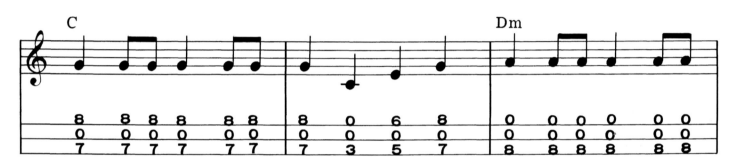

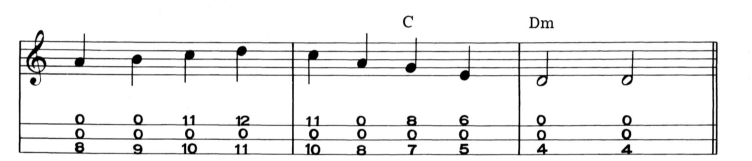

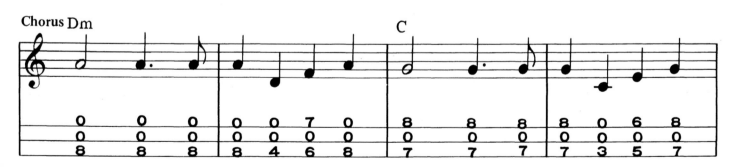

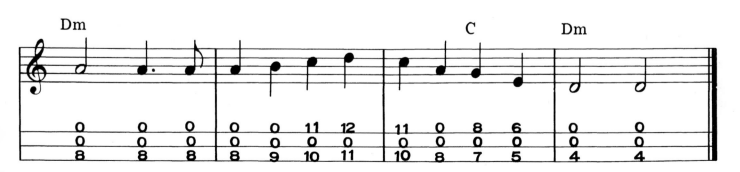

# EVERY NIGHT

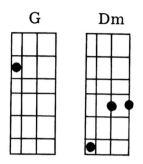

Mixolydian Mode

Ev -'ry night_____ when the sun goes down_____ Ev -'ry

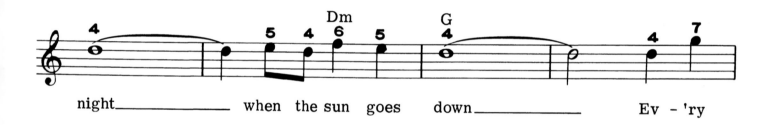

night_____ when the sun goes down_____ Ev - 'ry

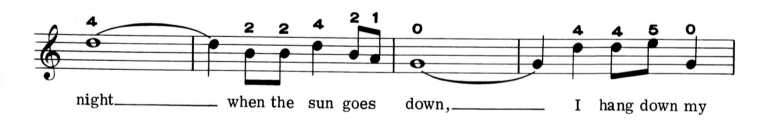

night_____ when the sun goes down,_____ I hang down my

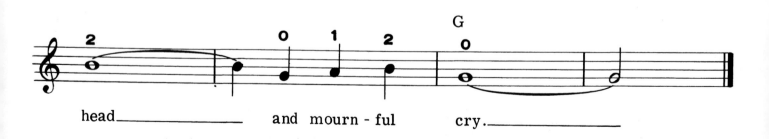

head_____ and mourn - ful cry._____

40

# EVERY NIGHT
## SOLO

Mixolydian Mode

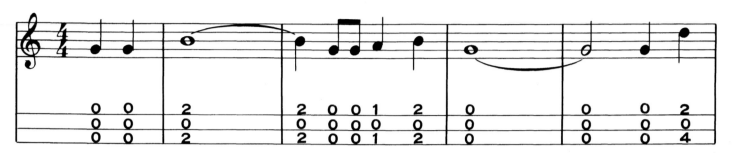

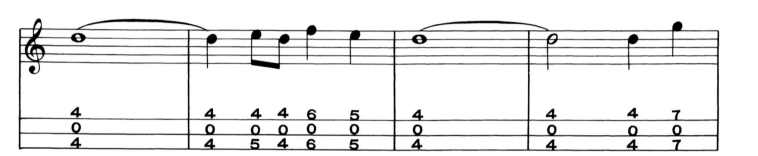

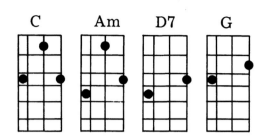

# THE FOGGY, FOGGY DEW

Ionian Mode

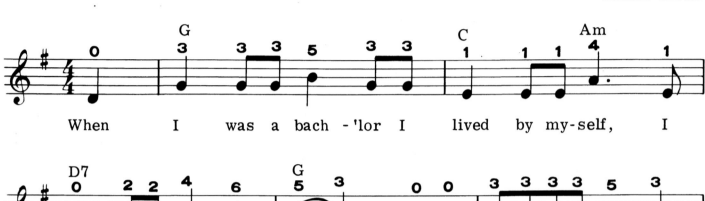

When    I    was a bach -'lor  I    lived    by my-self,        I

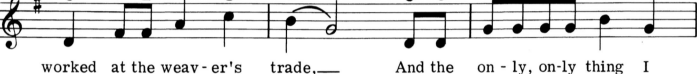

worked at the weav - er's    trade,____    And the    on - ly, on-ly thing  I

did    that was wrong was to    woo    a fair young    maid.        I

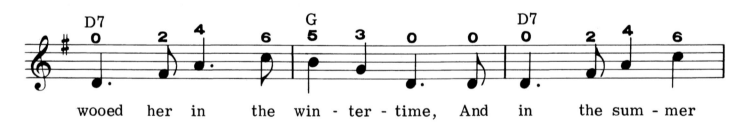

wooed    her in    the  win - ter - time,  And    in    the sum - mer

too,        And the    on-ly, on-ly thing  I    did    that was wrong was to

keep  her  from  the   fog - gy,  fog - gy        dew.

42

# THE FOGGY, FOGGY DEW
## SOLO

Ionian Mode

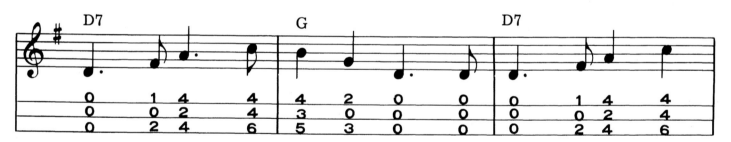

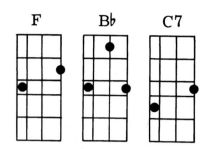

# FROGGIE WENT A-COURTIN'

Ionian Mode

Oh Frog-gie went a-court-in' and he did ride, A - huh,

Frog-gie went a-court-in' and he did ride A - huh,

Frog-gie went a-court-in' and he did ride, Sword and pis - tol

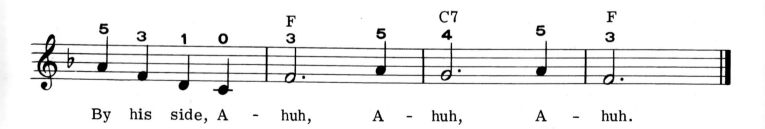

By his side, A - huh, A - huh, A - huh.

# FROGGIE WENT A-COURTIN'
## SOLO

Ionian Mode

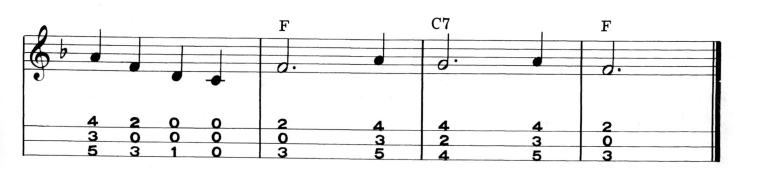

# GOLDEN SLIPPERS

Ionian Mode

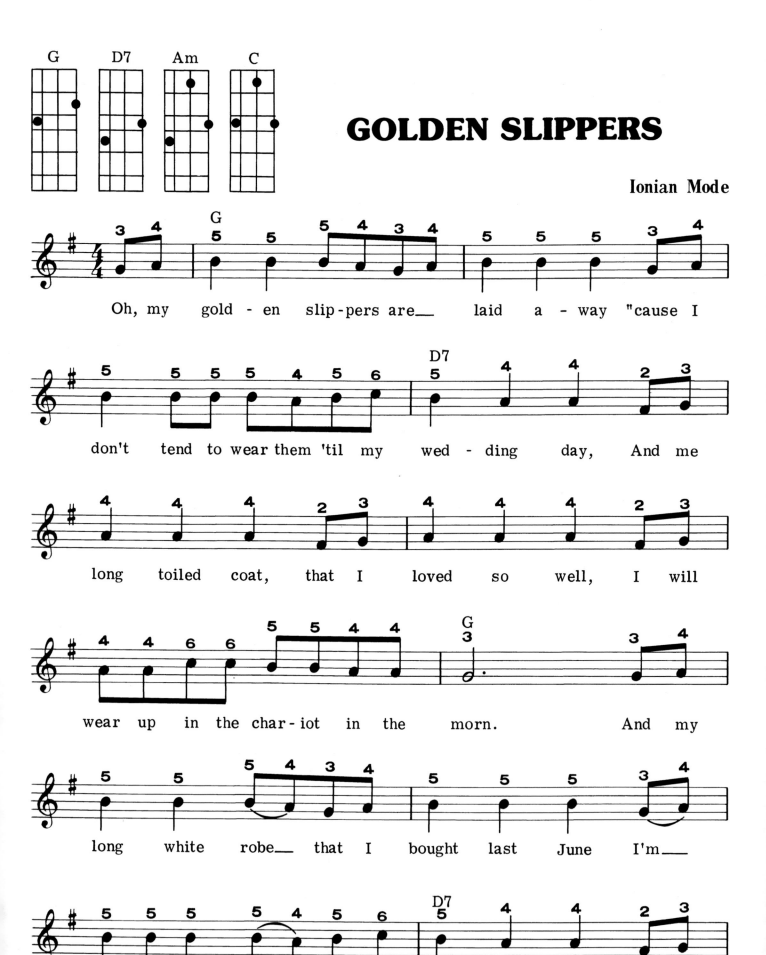

old gray horse that I used to drive, I will

hitch him to the char - iot in the morn

**Chorus**

Oh, them gol - den slip - pers Oh, them

gold - en slip-pers, Gold - en slip-pers, I'm go'- in to wear Be -

cause they look so neat. Oh, them gol-den slip-pers

Oh, them gol - den slip-pers gol - den slip-pers I'm

go'- in to wear to walk the gol - den street.

47

# GOLDEN SLIPPERS
## SOLO

Ionian Mode

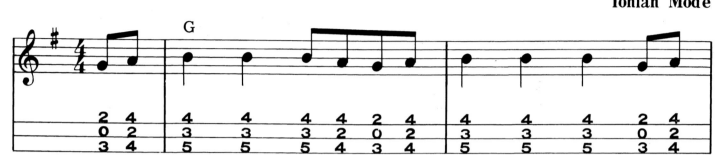

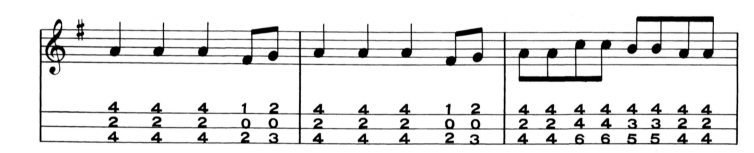

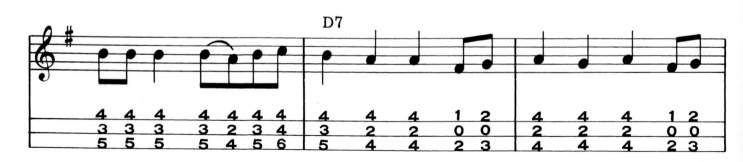

**Chorus**

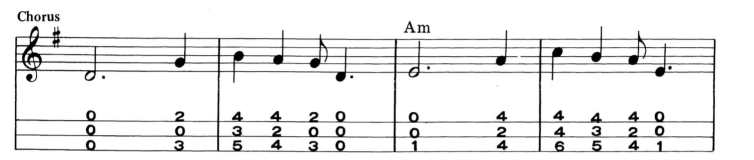

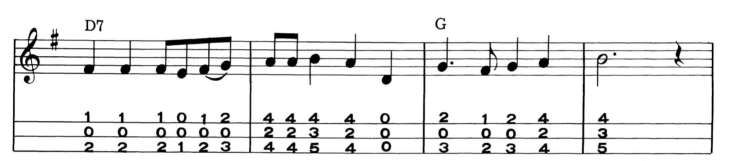

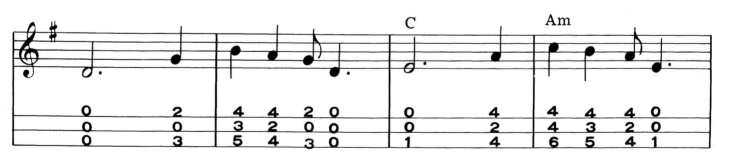

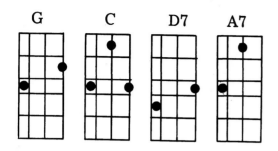

# GO TELL IT ON THE MOUNTAIN

Ionian Mode

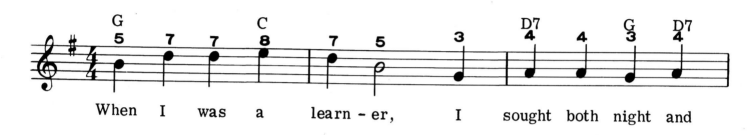

When I was a learn - er, I sought both night and

day, I asked the Lord to help me, and

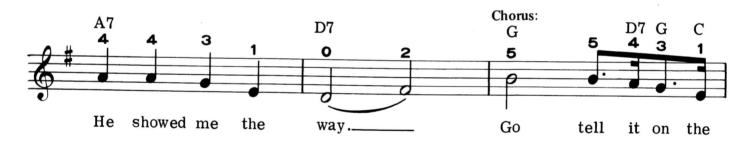

He showed me the way._____ Go tell it on the

moun - tains, O-ver the hills and ev' - ry - where,_____

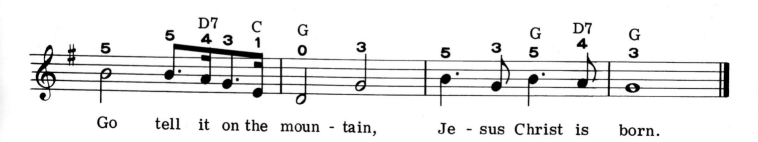

Go tell it on the moun - tain, Je - sus Christ is born.

# GO TELL IT ON THE MOUNTAIN

**SOLO**

Ionian Mode

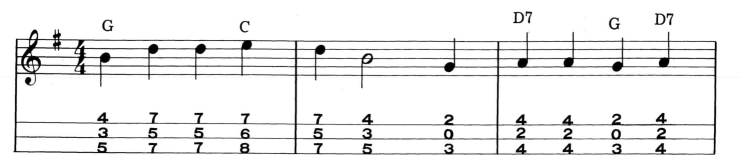

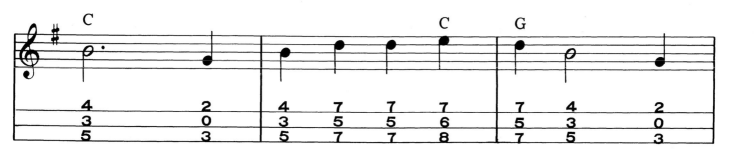

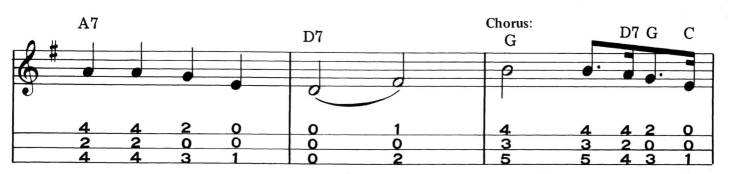

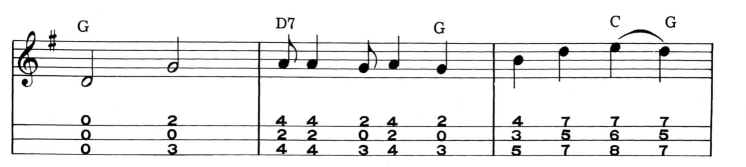

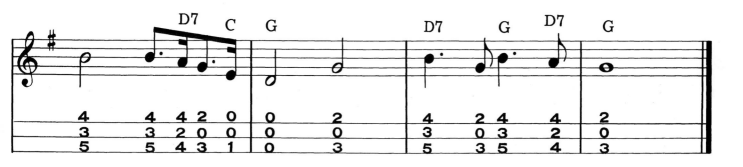

# GRANDFATHER'S CLOCK

Ionian Mode

My Grand-fath-er's clock was to large for the shelf, So it
stood nine-ty years on the floor. It was
Tall-er by half than the old man him-self though it
weighed not a pen-ny weight more. It was
bought on the morn of the day that he was born, And was

al - ways his plea - sure and joy, But it

stopped short nev - er to go a - gain, When the

old man died. Nine - ty years with - out slum - ber - ing

Tick, Tock, Tick Tock; His life sec - onds num - ber - ing

Tick, Tock, Tick Tock; It stopped short

nev - er to go a - gain, when the old man died.

# GRANDFATHER'S CLOCK
## SOLO

Ionian Mode

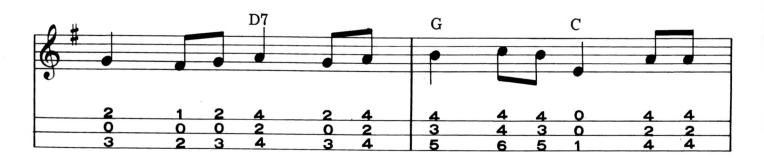

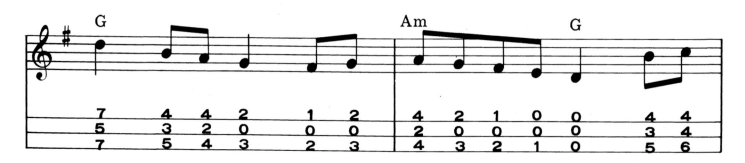

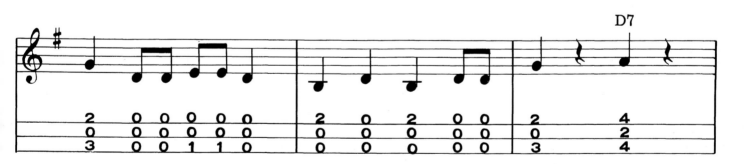

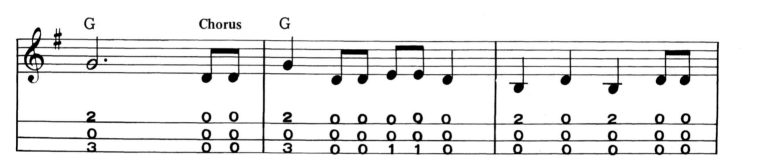

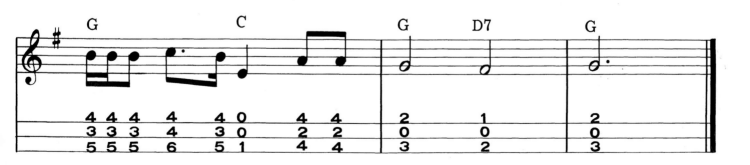

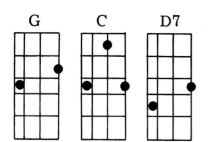

# I'VE GOT PEACE LIKE A RIVER

Ionian Mode

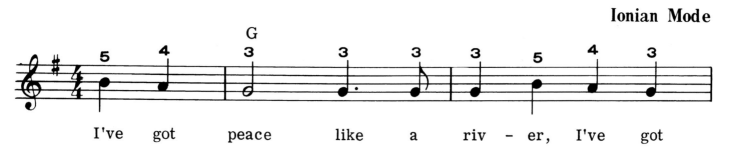

I've got peace like a riv - er, I've got

peace like a riv - er, I've got peace like a

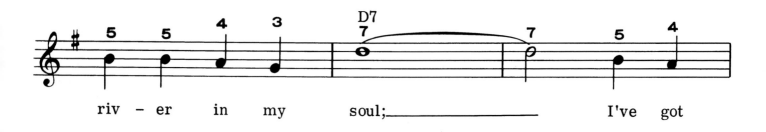

riv - er in my soul;_____ I've got

peace like a riv - er, I've got peace like a riv - er, I've got

peace like a riv - er in my soul._____

# I'VE GOT PEACE LIKE A RIVER
## SOLO

Ionian Mode

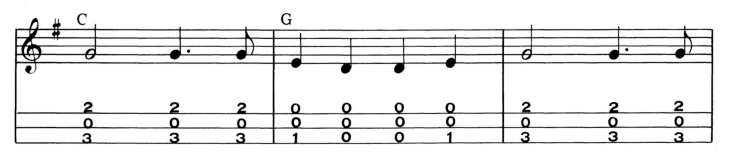

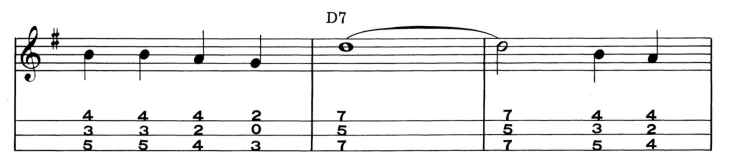

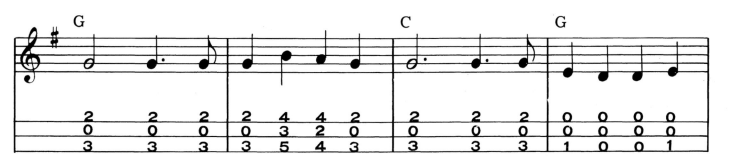

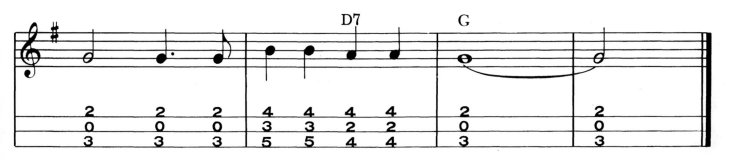

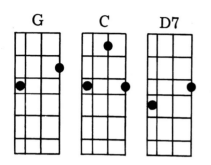

# LONDONDERRY AIRE

Irish Air
Ionian Mode

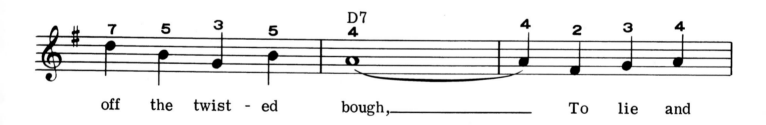

Would God I were the ten - der ap - ple

blos - som, \_\_\_\_\_ That floats and falls from

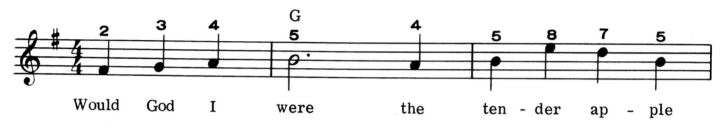

off the twist - ed bough, \_\_\_\_\_ To lie and

faint with - in your silk - en bos - om, \_\_\_\_\_

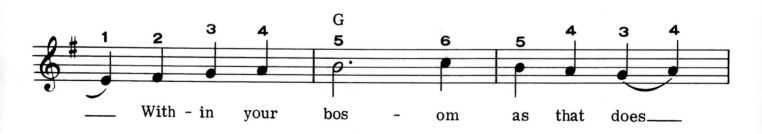

\_\_ With - in your bos - om as that does\_\_

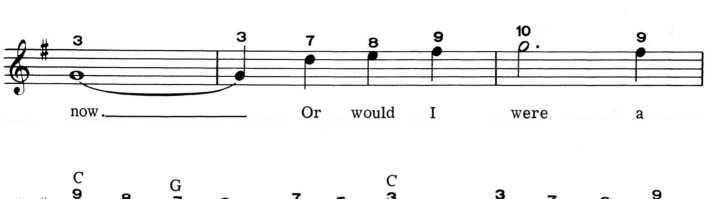

now._____ Or would I were a

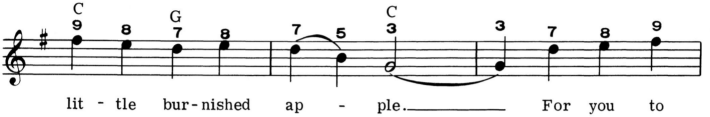

lit - tle bur - nished ap - ple._____ For you to

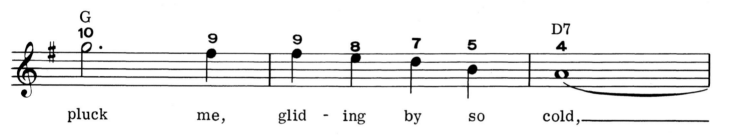

pluck me, glid - ing by so cold,_____

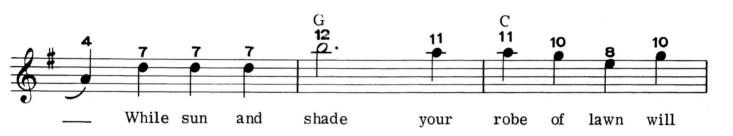

\_\_ While sun and shade your robe of lawn will

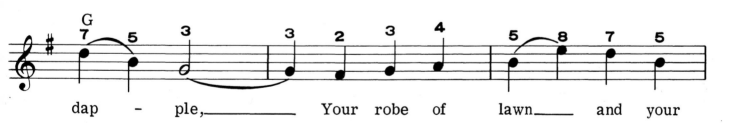

dap - ple,_____ Your robe of lawn\_\_\_ and your

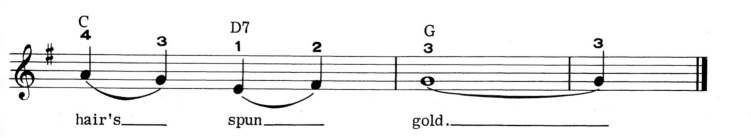

hair's\_\_\_ spun\_\_\_\_\_ gold._____

# LONDONDERRY AIRE
## SOLO

Ionian Mode

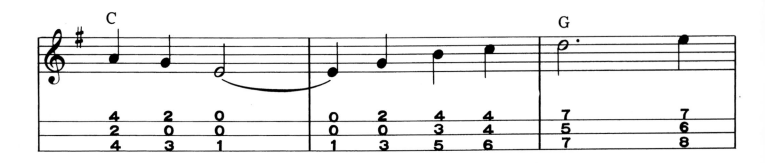

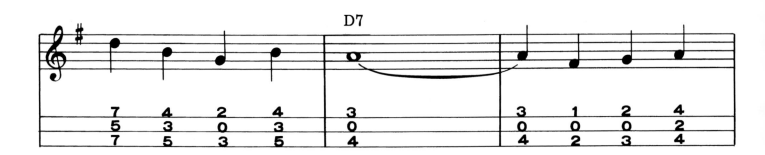

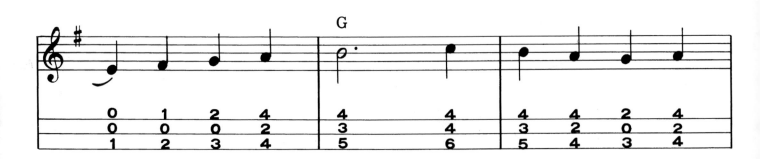

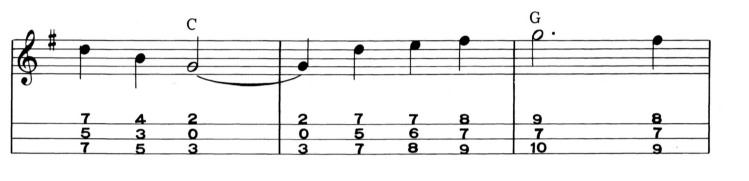

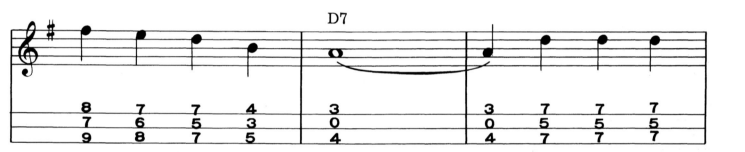

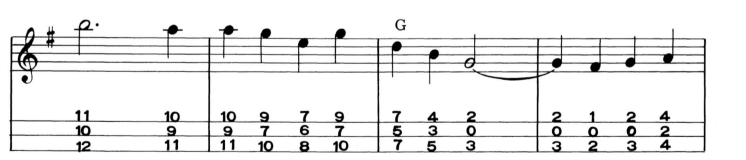

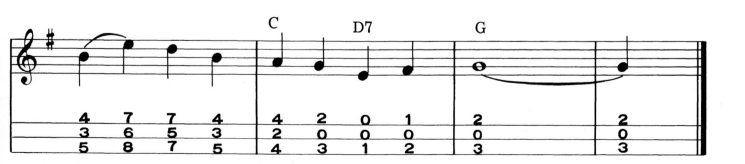

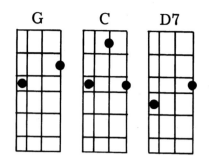

# OH MARY DON'T YOU WEEP

Ionian Mode

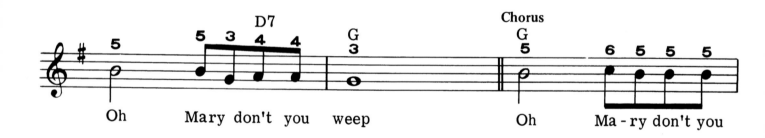

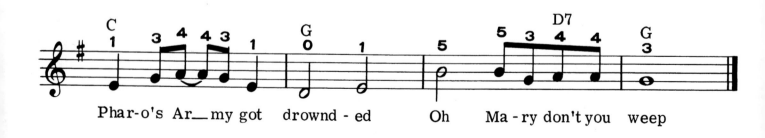

# OH MARY DON'T YOU WEEP
## SOLO

Ionian Mode

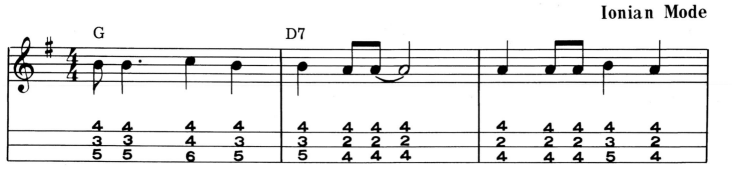

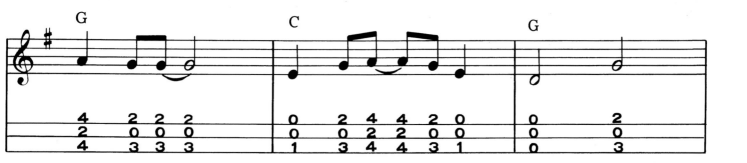

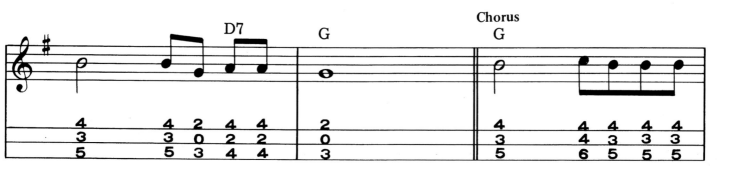

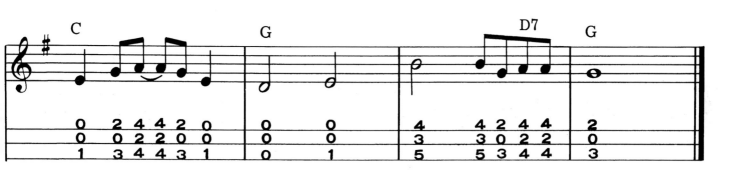

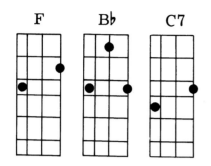

# OLD ROSIN THE BEAU

Ionian Mode

I live for the good of the na - tion, My sons are all grow - ing

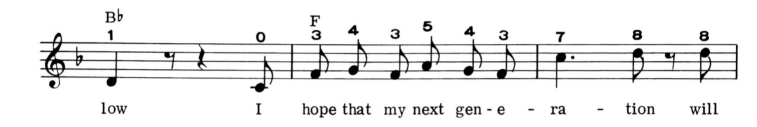

low        I hope that my next gen - e - ra - tion will

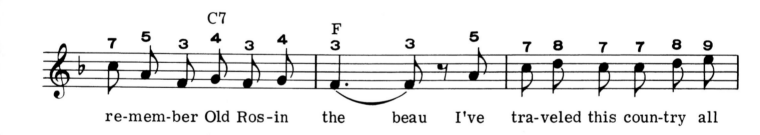

re-mem-ber Old Ros-in the beau I've tra-veled this coun-try all

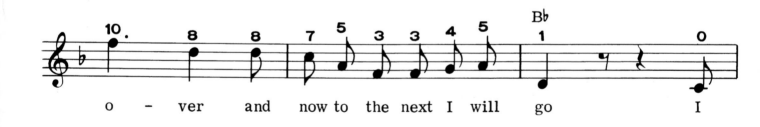

o — ver and now to the next I will go        I

know that good quarters a - wait me to wel-come Old Ros-in the Beau___

# OLD ROSIN THE BEAU
## SOLO

Ionian Mode

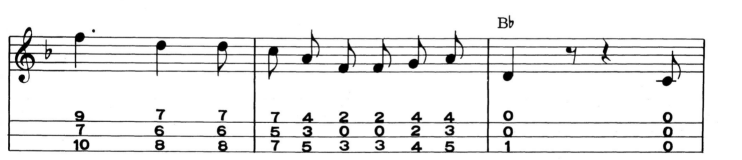

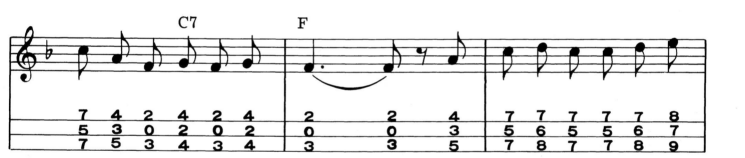

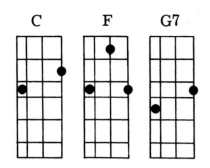

# ON TOP OF OLD SMOKEY

Ionian Mode

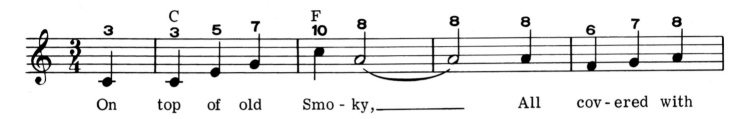

On top of old Smo-ky,_____ All cov-ered with

snow._____ I lost my true lov-er_____ from

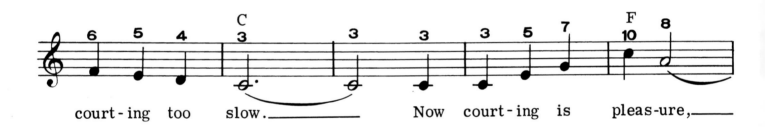

court-ing too slow._____ Now court-ing is pleas-ure,\_\_\_\_

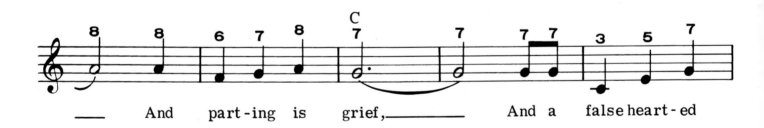

\_\_\_ And part-ing is grief,_____ And a false heart-ed

lov-er_____ is worse than a thief.\_\_\_\_

# ON TOP OF OLD SMOKEY
## SOLO

Ionian Mode

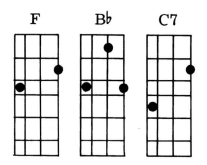

# RIDDLE SONG

Ionian Mode

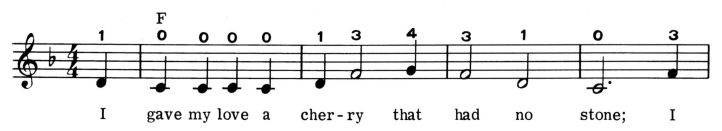

I gave my love a cher-ry that had no stone; I

gave my love a chick-en that had no bone; I

told my love a sto-ry that had no end; I

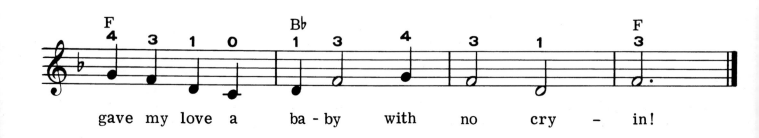

gave my love a ba-by with no cry - in!

# RIDDLE SONG
## SOLO

Ionian Mode

# SALLY GOODIN

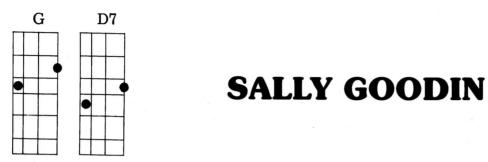

Ionian Mode

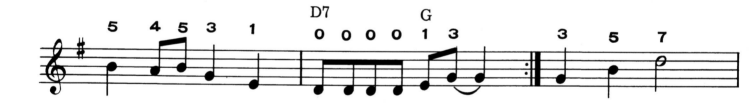

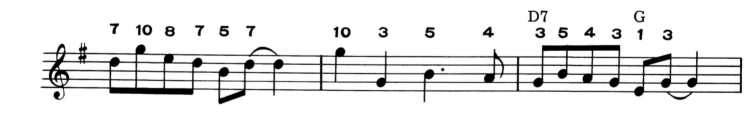

# SALLY GOODIN
## SOLO

Ionian Mode

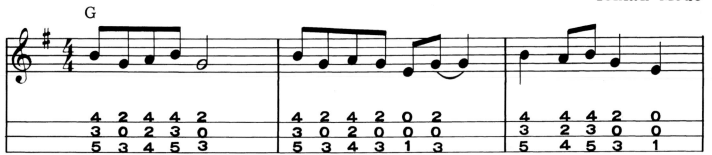

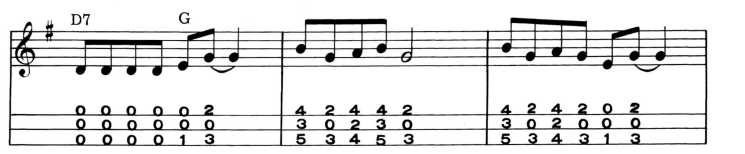

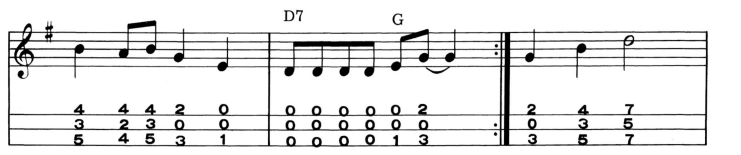

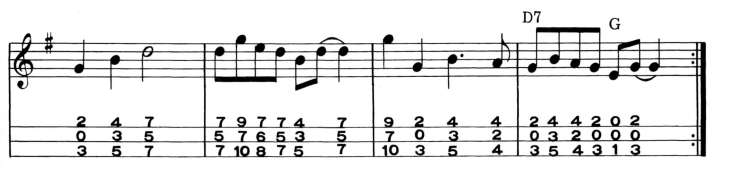

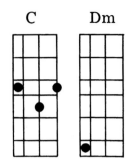

# SCARBOROUGH FAIR

Dorian Mode

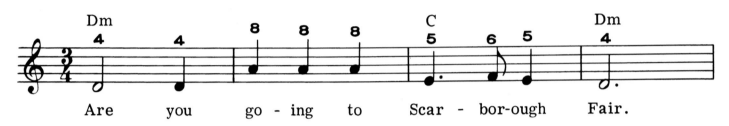

Are you go - ing to Scar - bor - ough Fair.

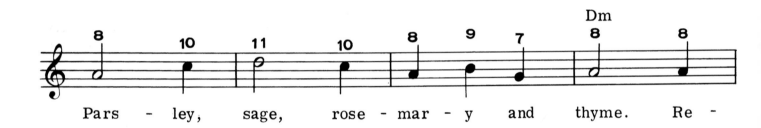

Pars - ley, sage, rose - mar - y and thyme. Re -

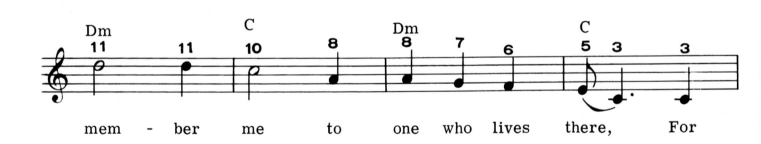

mem - ber me to one who lives there, For

once she was a true love of mine.

# SCARBOROUGH FAIR
## SOLO

Dorian Mode

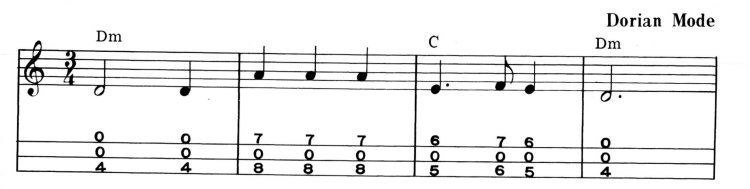

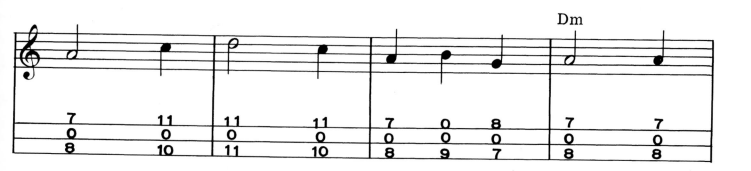

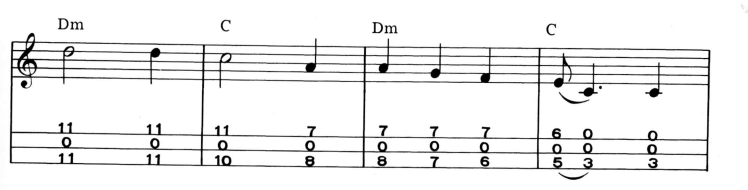

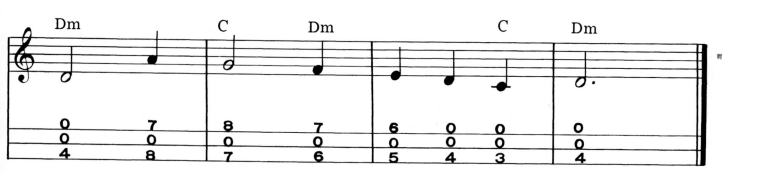

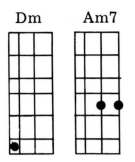

# SHADY GROVE

Dorian Mode

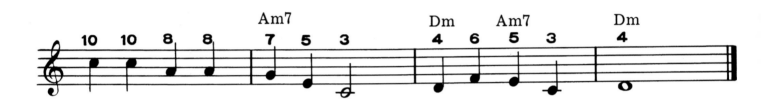

# SHADY GROVE
## SOLO

Dorian Mode

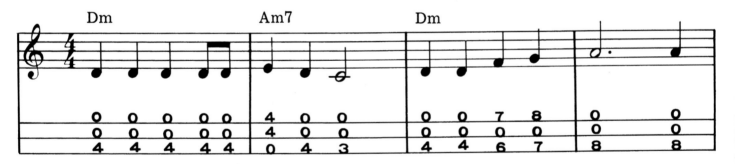

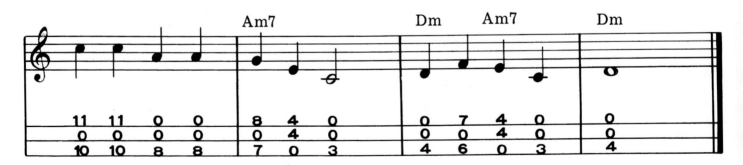

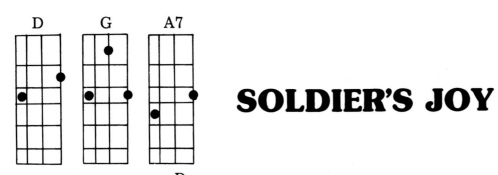

# SOLDIER'S JOY

Ionian Mode

# SOLDIER'S JOY
## SOLO

Ionian Mode

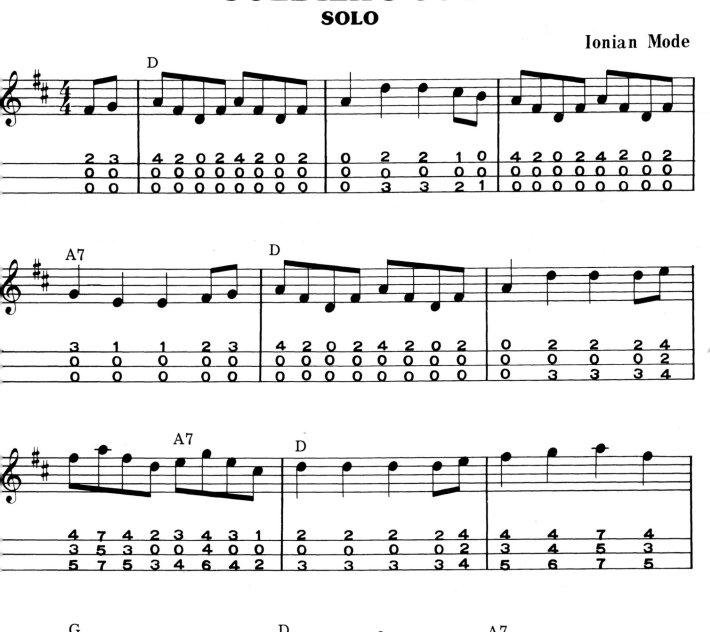

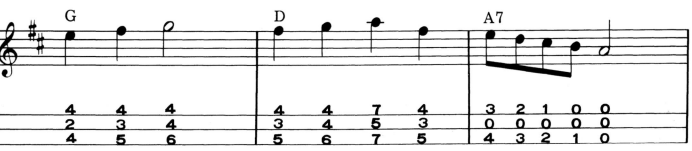

# THERE IS A BALM IN GILEAD

*Ionian Mode*

There is a balm in Gil - e - ad, to make the wound - ed whole, There is a balm in Gil - e - ad, to heal the sin sick soul.

Some - times I feel dis - cour - aged, And think my work's in vain, But then the Ho - ly Spir - it Re - vives my soul a - gain.

# THERE IS A BALM IN GILEAD
## SOLO

Ionian Mode

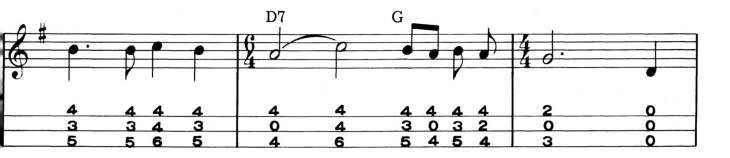

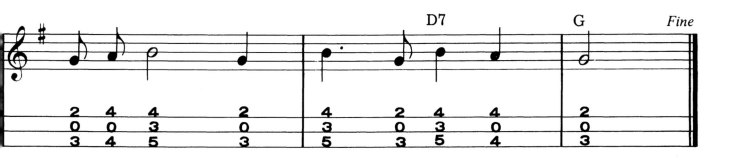

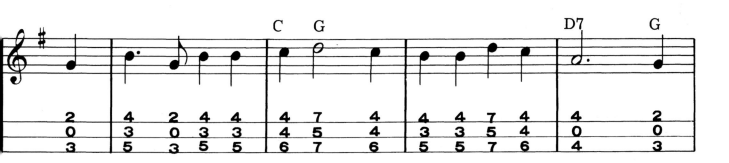

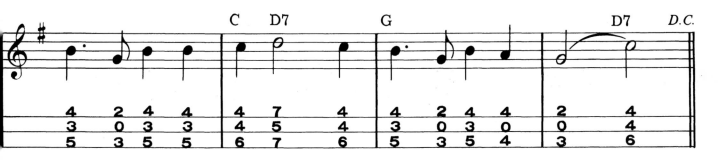

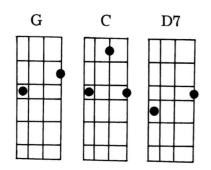

# THE WATER IS WIDE

Ionian Mode

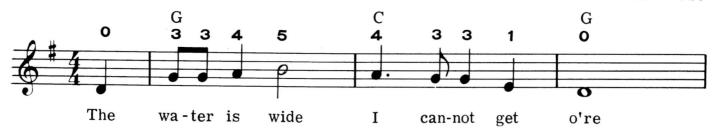

The wa-ter is wide I can-not get o're

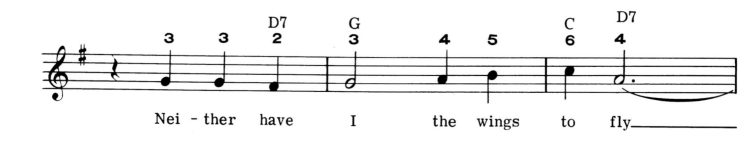

Nei - ther have I the wings to fly____

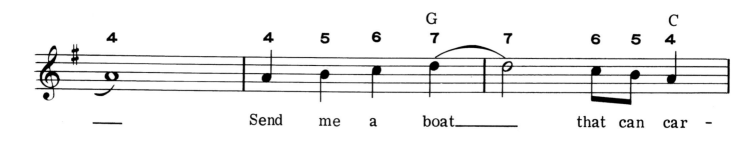

____ Send me a boat____ that can car -

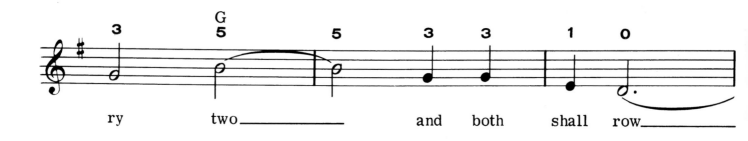

ry two____ and both shall row____

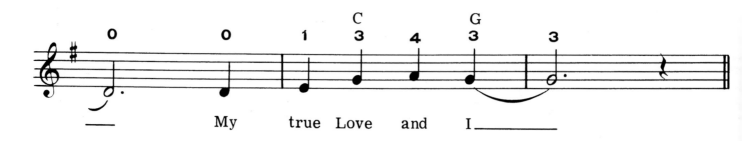

____ My true Love and I____

# THE WATER IS WIDE
## SOLO

Ionian Mode

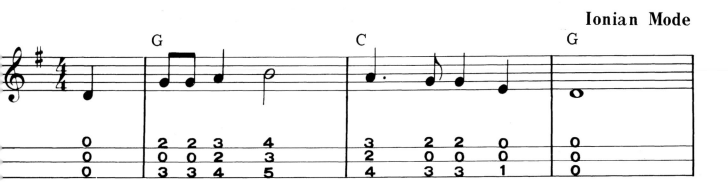

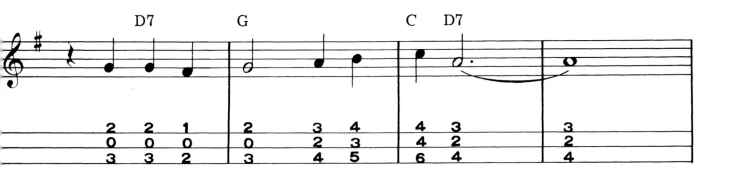

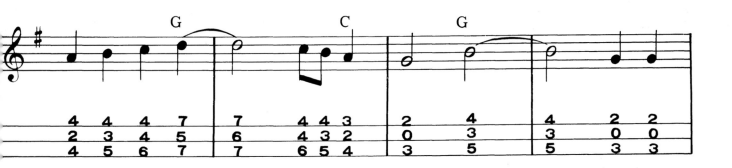

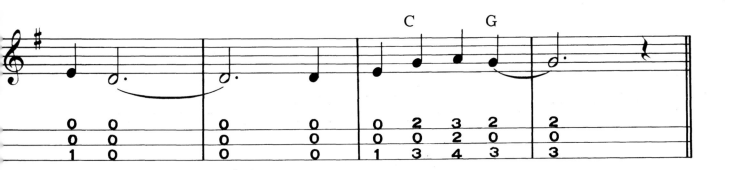

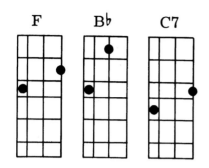

# WABASH CANNONBALL

Ionian Mode

From the great At-lan-tic O-cean to the great Pa-cif-ic

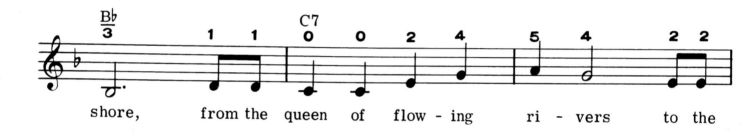

shore, from the queen of flow-ing ri-vers to the

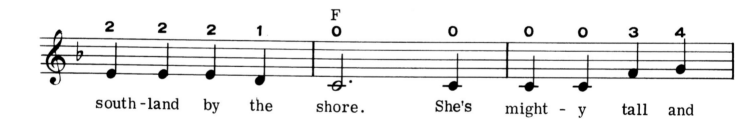

south-land by the shore. She's might-y tall and

hand-some and quite well known by all.

She's the com-bi-na-tion of the Wa-bash Can-non-ball.

82

# WABASH CANNONBALL
## SOLO

Ionian Mode

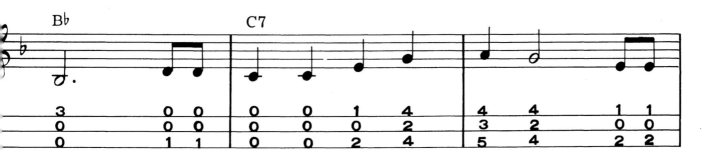

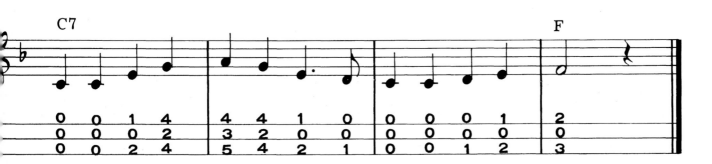

# WILDWOOD FLOWER

Ionian Mode

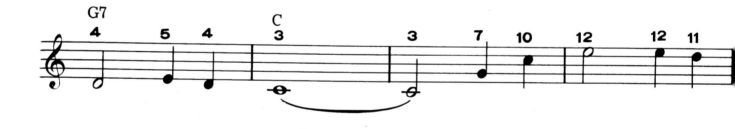

# WILDWOOD FLOWER
## SOLO

Ionian Mode

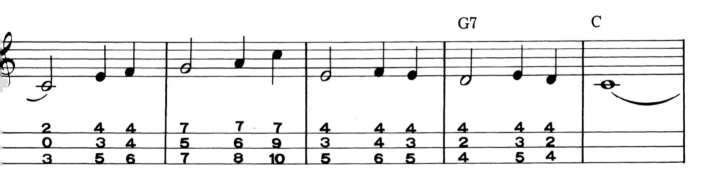

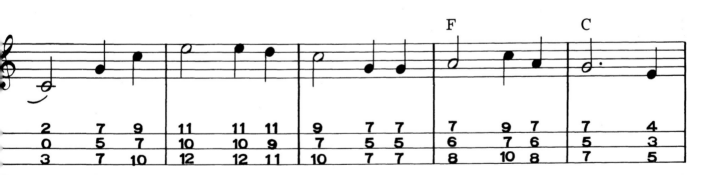

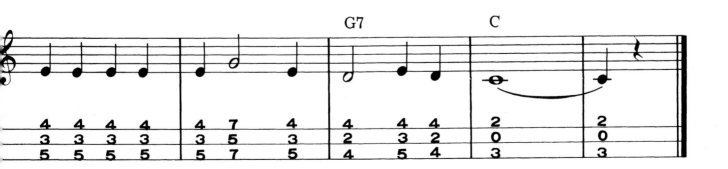

# WHEN THE SAINTS GO MARCHING IN

Ionian Mod[e]

Oh when the saints_____ go march-ing In,_____

Oh when the saints go march - ing In,_____

Oh, Lord I want to be in that num-ber,_____

When the saints go march - ing In._____

# WHEN THE SAINTS GO MARCHING IN
## SOLO

Ionian Mode